How to Avoid
Police Brutality

STELLA EBURUO

Printed in the United States of America
First Printing: November 2023

DEDICATION

To my three children, Jennifer, Chidiebere, and
Patrick, and my husband, Patrick. I Love you -

CONTENTS

ACKNOWLEDGMENTS

Mayor Baraka for helping to clean up my city, Newark. He helped in fighting and in reducing crime in Newark, New Jersey, and helped with challenges and developments.

SO MANY SHOTS WERE FIRED

So many shots were fired by the police; so many also should have been avoided. So many people died; so many deaths also should have been avoided. When somebody gets shot, it could lead to death, paralysis, lifetime injury or leave biggest scars that carry on for generations. So, my advice is "safety first, obey before complaining."

Life is the most precious thing that you cannot buy with influence or any amount of money. Life is sweet and worth protection, but we do not realize it until it is too late, heavily hurt or lost. When I look at the picture, I can see people of color, specifically black people, as the most victimized of this issue each time it happens out there in the news on television. It breaks my heart. It drives me to start thinking about what can help us, the community, with this situation to navigate this every other time occurrence, how or what can be done, for us and the police to communicate friendly and peacefully, to stop this brutal, untimely, and unnecessary loss of lives in the hands of police officers.

There are many ways we can avoid police brutality whenever there is a stop or an encounter. Police brutality means, the not wanted, excessive, and, sometimes, against-the-law use of force by the police officers in this country and in some other parts of the world against people. Or it can also be referred to as a situation in which police officers exercise excessive force and mistreatment against a person. Forms of police brutality have been seen in the manner of beating, torture, assault, murder, heating people with a stick, and battery.

Around the world, and here in the United States of America, the group that has been affected by this police brutality most is the black and brown-skinned, often called "people of color." On May 3, 1963, in Birmingham, Alabama, during the civil rights movement, civil rights demonstrators were mistreated by the police. They were attacked by police dogs. There were mistreatments, including harassment, which included false arrests, intimidation, and physical and verbal abuse.

The consequences of police brutality include constant violence in the communities, cities, and country in general. It causes hate and unrest in society, involving citizens in uniform and not in uniform turning on each other. Losing lives left and right or getting permanently injured can lead to war, where the police and citizens are not listening to each other or trying to harm each other. Police brutality can affect even the government budget. When police cars and buildings are being burned down or damaged, that is a lot of money going out from the government pocket for replacement or repair of those damaged properties. Therefore, we must, everyone, do everything in the country and around the world, in our power to avoid and prevent police brutality. We can protest about the shooting and killing that follows it, but not with violence.

Respectfully speaking, being seen out there stealing, looting, burning down government and private buildings, fellow citizens' businesses, and churches, hurting and killing other innocent people, including police officers is surely not the type of action that can fix this, even though these are the very things that are done to us.

WHILE PROTESTING

While protesting, it is not okay to block people who are going to their businesses, such as truck drivers, who may be delivering groceries, taxi drivers, or regular drivers going to work or the hospital. They might not know there is a protest going on yet get in trouble. The police officers should also be allowed to pass through without being blocked.

To also protest safely, print T-shirts for protesters and do not block the road for anyone, for that can highjack the reason or reasons for the protest, not to be labeled violent protesters, because if the protesters block the road, it could cost pregnant women who are rushing to get to the hospital or people with medical attention in general. It can also prevent fire trucks answering their call on time, people getting to work late or affecting their time and other plans they have because the road was blocked by protesters. Make a banner that says what you are protesting for and walk peacefully without blocking the traffic, that is safe for everyone, so people can go to their businesses without interruption. There is absolutely no reason for anybody to get hurt, die, or lose their vehicle due to a protest going on. Sit or stand safely for everyone stay in one place or move around, ring bell, beat drums, sing, and/or shout why you are protesting and eventually the message will surely get delivered to those it concerns.

We shall bring back the ways our ancestors did their protests, protective and peaceful. Dr. Martin Luther King Jr. and Honorable John Lewis did not spit at police officers or kill our little sisters and brothers; instead, they matched it with nonviolence, holding hands together with their signs that portrayed their reason for protesting, walking, and marching peacefully, and eventually, they listened to their request no matter how long it lasted. We can also protest by figuring it out on our own. We can sit in groups holding our signs without damaging anything. We can now apply the addition of positivity and subtraction of negativity in our lives and in our community. We can share ideas to bring an end to this untimely and unnecessary death of our men and women, including police officers.

THE JOB OF THE POLICE

The job of the police is to keep law and order, secure the community, investigate law violations, gather evidence, make arrests, and solve crimes. No one is supposed to die suddenly, only because of a stop by a police officer or an order from a police officer or a police officer who came to their house for a warrant. I believe in law and order. Order is meant to be kept, but when it is not kept, one can get in trouble. Order could be in your family in the form of everyone being in bed by 9:00pm, or while in school, you cannot use your cell phone in the classroom while the teacher is teaching.

The law of the land is an order in so many ways, and it has to be respected and obeyed. Policemen and policewomen are trained by the police force. They are part of the law enforcement of the country to keep law and order in the community and country in general, but they are also human beings like us. The only difference is their job title and responsibilities to make sure there is peace, security, and law and order.

There is good and bad in this world depending on your choice of belonging. There are bad apples and good apples, good people and bad people, and even good priests and bad priests in the church. There are good police and the possibility of bad police. I want my brothers and sisters and people of color out there to remember that these individuals have force at the end of their occupational name, police force. They are always very alert, sensitive, smart, and fast. Their look might be intimidating, but all of that has nothing to do with our lives and destiny. We are saving our lives, from this point on.

Let us do our best to make every interaction with the police end well, not end our lives. For any reason, if you are given an order by a police officer, and he/she gives an order to stop, please stop right away. Please, my suggestion is to obey and comply with every piece of order given to you. If the order is to put your hands up in the air, please do it right away. If the order is to drop the gun, knife, or weapon of any kind, please drop it right away. Obey before you complain because when they see that you obey, the obedience automatically de-escalates any reason that may have led to the encounter.

This is why first impressions matter. Compose yourself as a human being. Do not engage in an argument or a fight with the police. Show them that you are a gentle man/woman, and they will follow your lead. Remove the idea that the police are targeting black men or people of color and represent yourself by doing exactly what they ask you to do, and let the country see the police officer who will shoot you for obeying his command.

What if the police were given a description of a suspect, for instance, a guy who was wearing a white T-shirt and black pants? Do not forget, people can dress alike and look alike, and even cars can resemble each other. One might be wearing a white T-shirt and black pants around the area the description was given. It is reasonable that the officer will stop the guy and ask some questions. Obviously, it is not the person of interest, but for a peaceful end, you should allow the officer to ask his questions. Do not run away from the police, resist, or reach for or point a gun at the police, even if you are a gun owner.

Guns are meant for protecting yourself from danger, not using them against the police or flaring them on the police. Again, start it right to end it right. At every approach or encounter by the police, patiently say what you know only, and do not say what you do not know. Assuming you have a weapon or something that does not belong to you in your car, do not panic or reach for anything. Remember, the police are watching for any movement. Once they stop you, exercise patience. If you did something wrong, the worst that might happen is getting in trouble, paying a fine, or spending some time in a correctional facility. It shouldn't cost you your life.. If well behaved, it can only come with a warning or possibly a pardon by a police officer, and also, you earn respect for yourself.

It is said that salutation is not love, but it is a good thing to salute. It reduces tension. It demands respect for both parties. It is a simple way to tell a police officer, "We are not enemies. I recognize you are doing your job. Thank you for what you are doing." There is nothing wrong with greeting a police officer with a smile on your face, "Good morning, sir," or "Good morning, ma'am," or "Hi, officer." Respect is reciprocal. If you respect and practice patience with the police, they will also respect and practice patience with you.

DO NOT RESIST ARREST

Do not resist arrest, for it is not the end of the world. Arrest resistance can turn into violence and become brutal. I have seen it over and over on television, guys, it does not work for us. Let people change ideas and stop resisting arrest, for a resisted provocative arrest, sometimes, turns deadly, or one becomes permanently injured, including innocent bystanders. Some people resist arrest by pointing flaring weapons at police, and some take off, causing police chases, dragging police around the communities. That kind of behavior contributes to bullets flying causing innocent bystanders to get shot or other accidents, which is dangerous to everyone, the police and the community.

On the other hand, the police should not shoot or kill a suspect or person of interest if he/she puts his/her hands up in the air, gun and weapon-free. It is unjustifiable for the police to shoot a weapon-free, hands in the air, non-threatening individual. It shows a little sign of surrender by the person in question to the police; therefore, the police should use their professionalism and expertise to handle the situation without discharging a bullet, especially if they are more than one, so each group will be safe. It is ideal for the government or police management to hire more police and make it mandatory to have more than two police officers at a time for any situation. Police well assigned will execute their job very well. If the police department will mandate answering any call or page in threes, more police officers at hand will back up now, not later.

It is reasonable that an officer moving toward an individual of interest should not discharge a bullet when they already have backup in case the suspect brings down his hand suddenly to use a weapon or fight the police. Also, the individual will likely keep his hands that are still up in the air because he sees how many officers are on the scene, which means a win for both the officers and the person in question; no bullets released, and everybody is safe.

INCLUSIVITY

Inclusivity of different people with different backgrounds from all walks of life, including the LGBTQ community, in the police force will help greatly in the avoidance of police brutality. Inclusivity will work well with the community. If we have people that look like us in the police force, advocating for us and educating us on how to live peacefully with policemen and policewomen, I truly believe there would be less animosity in the relationships we declare we are trying to build with the people that are supposed to be protecting us. For instance, policemen or policewomen who speak what people speak, who look like them or sound like them, can very much help ease and resolve misunderstandings and dissipate rising tension quickly and peacefully within most incidents.

This diversity and inclusion in the police force or hiring of more people of color can also help with solving problems easily. Assuming there is a 911 call in a black house or neighborhood, seeing somebody from their own community can help to solve any problem. "It's possible for an individual to communicate in a language that resonates with them, one they can comprehend, and to be receptive to guidance from someone who looks like them.". Most of the time, we see police officers in their uniforms in a fast-moving police car, rushing to save a life in one way or the other or sitting by the corner, making sure there is law and order in the community. We do not usually walk up to them to say hi or talk about visiting the police station.

Police can interact with people more in the community by attending their churches whenever they have a chance, just to show their faces and see their faces also. In their leisure time, they can watch or engage in recreational activities with the people in the community, games like soccer, basketball, football, or running relays, just to associate with kids in the city. This type of communication between the police and the community would allow for the development of strong relationships.

If a police officer dies, especially in a line of

duty, the people in the community should show concern and sympathize with the family. Visit the place he or she has fallen. Lay sympathy cards, flowers, or balloons. Write on cardboard and say thanks for his or her service, for protecting the community. If possible, the people in the community should attend the funeral service. If people in the community can call for a GoFundMe for money to help the family of the fallen police officer, that would be a good gesture and another way to express gratitude to a fallen hero.

EDUCATION IS POWER

"Education is power," said Nelson Mandela. Give us school choice and free education. It will be a tremendous opportunity in general especially for people of color. They will be educated in so many areas of profession, and I believe many will go in for a police force academy or take a police-job training course to make sure there is a good number of black and brown people in the police force. For a person of color and anyone it may concern, becoming a police officer will help tremendously in avoiding police brutality.

First, if you do not like what is going on, change it. When you know better, you do better. The person will be able to sit down at the table with other police officers or management to let them know what it feels like to be on the other side. Maybe he has experienced brutality or witnessed it. It can be debated, and there may be changes to any topic brought up. See something, say something. Nobody is perfect. If a police officer sees anything wrong on either or both sides of the police force or people in the community, he will be able to correct it firsthand. While doing his job, he will always practice good policing because he knows what it takes to survive and fix it. If any person out there has a question, he will be able to give a satisfactory answer.

Underdeveloped countries around the world have police force, why not America, the greatest country in the world. I call it the "giant of the world." I call it "the world power," "the last bus stop." America is freedom, a country if you have never been in it, you have not started. If you have never been to America, you are missing out. It's a place where the grace of God is flowing like milk and honey.

I AM STRONGLY AGAINST DEFUNDING

I am strongly against defunding the police. There are still good policemen and policewomen who are doing the right thing out there. If the police force is defunded, crime will go up. Crime will soar from cities that slashed police budgets. Shootings, violent protesters instead of peaceful protesters, murders, and other crimes will rise. There is never a good time to defund the police, especially our friends, in-laws, husbands, wives, cousins, parents, even strangers who are good policemen and policewomen. The world will not be cooler if we de-fund the police.

There are good apples and bad apples. There are so many superhero police out there and bad police who choose to make bad decisions on the job. Bad police are the only ones who use excessive force that causes the death of somebody who is not supposed to die in the first place, police who throw bad and insulting words to a person on the floor fighting for his/her dear life. No one wants to be bad, that is the reason why we must be prayerful to start and finish our jobs every day with positivity. Because one police misbehaving does not mean we have to counter or abolish the rest of the police or their jobs.

If possible, the police should check for anger management and treatment if there is a need. Police management should always hire enough workers. They should not manage to have fewer workers. They will be stressed out and it will affect their performance in the community they serve. Police departments should give the fullest warning or penalty to any officer who engages in misconduct on the job. That kind of reaction will be a reminder to other policemen and policewomen to be mindful of their jobs. Police officers are human beings like us. They have their families and responsibilities, and they are the best thing in the communities they serve. Of course, so many policemen and policewomen have done their job well and beyond. Yes, they police our community for the peace, security, and well-being of the people. They sometimes use dogs, some ride cars, bicycles, horses, fly helicopters when necessary, to ensure our safety in all aspects of our communal lives. They deserve to be protected.

Bulletproof vests for the police should be mandatory and the best model in the world for the best protection. They should always put on their vests and helmets that are bulletproof on their heads while commuting to the community or policing any area whether it is staying in one place in the car watching the traffic or standing on corners. The vests and the helmets will help to keep the police officers safe. A policewoman should have not died from bullets in her head. If she had a bulletproof helmet or if she had one or two more police officers in the car with her, perhaps her death could have been avoided.

Some police officers go the extra mile in perfecting their jobs. For instance, recently, a police officer was showing an African American boy how to ride a bicycle safely. Countless pregnant women have given birth on the highway road with the assistance of a police officer on duty. They have saved many pets, children, and adults from homes, burning buildings, kidnappers, etc. A three-week-old was saved from choking by the police when his/her mom called for help. The police help a lot when a family member is missing, especially the people with challenges from birth.

They come to our rescue when we have a burglary or conflict in the house or have problems with people whose chests are ten times bigger than ours or if we have to fight with people with intimidating sizes and looks. They do tremendous jobs during storms, snow, pandemic, hurricane, and emergencies. The police help us with evacuation if there is a bomb threat or fire. "Police officers play a role in preventing and deterring terrorism and responding, for example, to incidents like shootings.". The police will run toward the active scene while everybody will be running away from the scene for their dear lives. We cannot deny or underrate their act of heroism. The police help with emergency medical technicians if there is a serious accident. They help save lives in the communities by performing cardiopulmonary resuscitation. Once you dial 911 for the police, help will be on the way to assist you.

Some police officers have drowned while

trying to save us. There is so much they do for us. But also, the police are reformable. It is important to reform and retrain the police well when necessary. They are human beings who can still make mistakes or make bad choices. We all learn every day The only difference is that police officers were trained to use force sometimes in certain situations, but not excessive force. When somebody resists arrest, still, the police can do their job but not with the use of excessive force. The police can be penalized if they misuse their power also. They can be discredited and served warnings, pay a fine, serve prison time, or be dismissed, depending on the crime committed. The action should always serve as a reminder to perfect their job at all times; therefore, reform and retrain the police right.

The police should not make the mistake of shooting and killing a person who did not deserve to die or shooting and permanently injuring an individual. Where word of mouth could have solved the problem, they need to show more professionalism in that case. When it comes to our children, the police should be extra careful. Children do not know much yet. A child will always behave like a child. They can easily go for what they see, what they hear, or maybe, what they were told. If children misbehave around the police, it is not their fault because they do not do good or bad. Children misbehave around parents, too, not because they want to but because they don't really know what they are doing. So, to avoid a dent or questioned job performance, the police should figure out a safe way to handle children whenever they are involved so that everyone will be safe.

The police should understand that people still respect their uniforms and still have faith in them, so they should do their job with fairness, not favoritism. The police should not permit personal feelings while performing their job. They must avoid excessive force. Reforming the police should also include hiring more police officers. More criminals and less police will not favor the communities. The police are anti-crime, while criminals insist on violent crimes, people killings, auto theft, rape, assault, slashing, pushing and hitting, stealing, burning, and shoplifting. The police force should reform and retrain police officers appropriately on how to use force or no force in cases as simple as a traffic stop, counterfeit money use to more dangerous cases like shooting and robbery, or when there is a resisting of arrest.

The police can also retrain on abuse of power by the police officers. A beating by the police officers that will leave somebody with a fractured skull, missing teeth, broken bones, and brain injury or beat to death in a police car is a perfect example of police abuse of power and excessive use of force. A young man who is stopped by the police may not comply well because he is already afraid of police abuse of power, which leads to resistance of any kind, and the end result will be police brutality. The police need to work on their use of power.

TO AVOID POLICE BRUTALITY

To avoid police brutality, during a protest, police officers should ask for help if needed. It could be from their colleagues within the city or outside the city. This makes sure policemen and policewomen who are working, the people, and their protest are safe. Since the beginning of the police force, there have been police superheroes, policemen and policewomen, both dead and alive, who did or are still doing their jobs well. These are some of the police officers who served or are still serving our communities. These are Americas top cops: Superintendent David O'Neal Brown, Chief Darnell Henry, Detective Joseph Seals, Detective Miosotis Familia, Officer Ella French, Officer Brenna Hosey, Officer Tyler Luellen, Third Generation Sheriff Deputy Ryan Clinkunbroomer and former police officer Mayor Erick Adams. These names represent the whole family of the police force that I am not able to mention this time.

The police should also retrain how to

manage protesters. Mauling down protesters with a police car is not the solution. They should learn how to clear up protesters safely, maybe coming up with enough police officers to safely move protesters out of the road instead of one or two police officers in the police car to run through human beings. That is not a good work ethic. The police department can use all the police they have in the city and call for help from neighboring towns to help clear the protesters. It will look more professional than to do otherwise and look unprofessional as people got hurt in the community. Police should also allow protesters or demonstrators to exercise their rights. They should not shoot or kill protesters. For example, in some other countries including African countries, people are being killed, beaten, harassed, jailed, or bombed from the air because they want to protest. It is the right of people to voice their opinions anywhere in the world.

To avoid police brutality and protest, demonstrations should be free and safe around the world, not interrupted by the police, instead of being protected by the police. Ban assault rifles and magazines for ordinary individuals or citizens out there. These types of guns should only be managed by the police and military. They do a lot of damage easily due to the many rounds it can generate in a little amount of time. It does not belong to our roads, not in the hands of our young people and, most importantly, not in the hands of criminals.

The gun buyback program is another important factor to help with the reduction of guns in general in our communities. Too many guns out there cause the communities to live in fear of witnessing crimes while running their everyday activities. Only a person who has a gun can reach for it. Only a person who has a gun at hand can fire it or shoot an officer or anybody out there. I have seen it time after time, police holding a gun and suspects or people in question holding a gun never end well. In most cases, it is very dangerous.

Our cities and communities are turning into war zones with frequent shootings followed by hurts and deaths. It is going to take a collaboration to deal with this problem between young people, families, cities, communities, churches, and the police. Before the police release bullets, they should do everything in their power to intentionally talk people out of resisting arrest and urge them to put hands up in the air and drop the weapon. Word of mouth, being used most of the time to solve these problems, will be a positive improvement in our communities. As a black woman, I have concerns with our children catching up with bullets every day: one-year-old, four-year-old, six-year-old, ten-year-old, sixteen-year-old. Guns are not favoring anyone, including us. They are killing us. Who are we going to hand over the torch in the future if these children keep dying of bullets? They are our leaders of tomorrow. Therefore, my suggestion will be to make a turn back, put down the guns, and let us look for the solution, the head of the table.

DO SOMETHING

Get an education if you can. Take a low-paying job if you are able or even take up a sport. You have to do something to keep busy and stay out of trouble. And keep voting until we get at the head of the table, or we vote for someone who is ready to support us a hundred percent. Maybe we will then live in a world that is gun-free, where no one will die of gunshot or be permanently injured due to gunshot or suffer from police brutality.

Young people, it is time to get up and start going to church to constantly hear the Word of God, for the beginning of a good life is found in the reverence of God. If you do not go to church, it is not a problem. Doing good is my religion and solution. If the police do good, and the people in the community do good, deaths, permanent injuries, and all kinds of losses associated with gunshots will be a case closed. It will gradually and finally end. Pursue kindness and loyalty toward your friends, family, the community, and the police.

Parents should constantly remind their young ones to abstain from unlawful gun use or ownership. Reducing the presence and use of illegal guns in our communities and cities is the most important factor. Too much of everything is bad, they say. In order to reduce the illegal firearms in society and promote a safer environment, the police can consider offering incentives such as cash rewards and gifts to individuals who voluntarily surrender their guns. This should be done without any intimidation, questioning, or threat of penalties or arrests. Give people money in exchange for their guns. The attraction of the money can cause some people to swap their guns for money. You can also consider Swapping their guns for electronics one can enjoy. Maybe even exchange guns with pre-paid cell phones, the payment of a cell-phone bill, or any bill of their choice. Swap guns with tickets to watch movies or enjoy outdoor activities. Swap AK-47s and magazines for even bigger prizes. You can hold and enjoy money, gifts, or a cell phone instead of holding a gun that can be deadly or put you in trouble and behind bars. No gun, no shooting. No shooting, no one will die of gunshot or have gunshot wounds.

Above all, activities reducing the number of guns in the community and the danger it poses should be the number one priority, the most important and urgent one to tackle. With guns being mishandled, even children are not safe while sleeping in their room. Guns bought recklessly will be handled recklessly and used recklessly. A world with heavy gun control would have been the best world, but before we get there, something has to be done now.

Heavy gun control is widely needed today. Be a loyal friend and a peacemaker today. It is always good to have a fair share, but if your brother or friend cheated on you on anything, maybe money, do not shoot or pull the trigger on him, for you do not know the last destination of that bullet. Instead, stop being a friend with him or her, stop the business with him or her.

LET ALL OF US, TOGETHER, ENJOY THIS SPORT IN THE GREATEST COUNTRY IN THE WORLD. WE ARE BLESSED TO BE IN THIS COUNTRY. WE HAVE TO DO EVERYTHING IN OUR POWER TO MAINTAIN OUR SPORT. IF WE PUT DOWN THE SWORD, GUN, AND KNIFE AND CARE AND PROTECT EACH ORDER, WE SHALL CONTINUE TO MULTIPLY IN NUMBERS, NOT REDUCING, AND BEFORE WE KNOW IT, WE WILL BE AT THE HEAD OF THE TABLE FASTER THAN WE THINK.

THOROUGH BACKGROUND CHECK

I believe there should be a thorough background and identification check for people buying guns, licenses, and there should also be a deep look into presented identification cards to determine their validity. I think it is super important to consider the appropriate age and mental health condition of a person purchasing a gun. I suggest that lawmakers should tighten the law when it comes to background checking. When it comes to buying guns, they should ask for a doctor's note clarifying that one is mentally healthy to use a gun.

Many a time, there has been a mass murder, whether in the casino, school, church, supermarket, movie theater, or other places. In most cases, the motive has been related to or due to mental illness. So, it is high time we propose the motion for a medical or doctor's note clarifying that one is mentally healthy to bear arms or carry a gun because a mentally ill person holding a gun can shoot anybody, including police

officers or people in the community. Shooting a
police officer will always attract police brutality.

There should be a massive penalty for gun-
shop owners who do not follow the rules or
buyers who break the law. Keeping guns or
firearms in the house is mainly for protecting the
family but should be carefully done because,
sometimes, the house includes a husband, wife,
children, extended family, and friends who are
visiting, babysitter, and caregiver. Guns must be
secured in a safety box or stored where they can
be locked safely. When a gun owner refuses to
secure his/her guns in safe manner to ensure that
kids cannot reach guns and use them carelessly to
hurt themselves, take guns to school to hurt
innocent school kids, schoolteachers, janitors, or
family members, that gun owner should pay a big
penalty and lose their gun ownership for a long
time or indefinitely. When people fail to protect
others, they must consider that they are also
failing to protect themselves.

A two-year-old, for example, allegedly
shoots his parents after finding a loaded gun on
the nightstand. This is a possibility when a gun

owner doesn't store their firearm properly.
Another example is a sixth grader who brought a
gun to her middle school. She shot and wounded
two students and a custodian and then was
disarmed by a teacher. In addition to an already
tragic situation, she could have done that to a
police officer, which could have led to brutality. A
three-year-old accidentally shot herself and
eventually died from the gunshot because the gun
was not protected properly by the owner, so
many children of different ages have fallen victim
to unsecured guns.

It is extremely important for gun owners to
properly protect their guns, for it also means
protecting many lives. Sometimes the
unprotected guns, by the owners, ends up in our
streets in the wrong hands of bad people and
criminals, contributing to the wrongful death of
our heroes, the men and women in the police
force, and the innocent citizens in the community
minding their businesses; or it could cause police
brutality if a gun picked up from a gun owner is
used to threaten a police officer.

Ban gun black-market sales. This type of

buying and selling guns will multiply the already growing guns in the cities, putting guns in the wrong hands of criminals, mentally ill, and drug abusers. People with anger management issues should not handle guns; it is dangerous for themselves and other people around them. If one can pull a gun on a fast-food worker through the fast-food window because of a wrong order, then he will shoot somebody who has a different opinion from him. It can attract the police chase, which is dangerous, both on land and air.

Imposing a big penalty on illegal gun buybacks and the gun black market will seriously reduce the amount of unnecessary and illegal guns out there that are causing unnecessary deaths and hurt every day. It will scare people from practicing this type of business and reduce the risk, and number of guns out there, and the danger that it contributes and poses every day. People in the city should treat 911 calls or call for police help the same way they do when they call a doctor. This means when calling 911, be ready to let the operator know descriptions and the exact reason for calling. But more importantly, if the person they are calling about is mentally ill, notify him/her right away.

The police shooting twenty-one gunshots at a mentally ill person is not justifiable. It is justifiable that the suspect is handled with extra caution because he is even more dangerous to himself. The police knowing that information when they are paged is very important. Police officers not knowing is different. If the police are notified about any mental challenges, they will apply their professionalism properly, using their words, a taser if necessary, BUT no excessive force, saving the suspect and not hurting the suspect severely and also avoiding the death of the suspect or police.

The 911 caller should always tell the operator if the person of interest is armed so that they will send adequate help, and everybody will be safe at the end of the day. examples of any harmful object: gun, knife, bottle, rock, hammer, or rod. Fake 911 calls should carry a heavy penalty. A lot of police officers have died due to this act, and it is not acceptable. People making fake calls are causing confusion for the police and the community because it's hard to tell when a real emergency is happening. It requires a big heavy fine. A fake 911 call is useless and can stir up big problems. When the police are sent on a wild goose chase, they miss a chance to deal with another important task. It can lead to losing police officers who are doing their job and are supposed to go back home to their families. During these chases, people might get hurt or even lose their lives, and this could have been prevented if it weren't for fake calls. No one should play with their lives or the government's time.

Without a doubt, choke holds should be banned. It means police mistreatment, which includes the physical restraint by a police officer when dealing with the people in the community. Strikes on the head, excessive kneeling on the neck, hitting with a stick, any interaction that is lethal should be banned. What if the person in question is suffering from a respiratory problem or health issue in general? What if the person is innocent? Even if they aren't innocent, this type of abuse is unnecessary. More than ever, the police should use professionalism in conducting their jobs.

An arrest can be conducted without using excessive force or resorting to a chokehold, as this technique has the potential to be fatal.. Police officers should not punch or beat a person that has been handcuffed. Police stations should be built in rural and suburban areas so that people in the community can have policemen and policewomen nearby in their uniforms all the time. To have them close is supposed to give you a sense of security, not fear. Every now and then, you might spot police officers shopping for fruits or lunch at the supermarket. When you see police and their cars outside the police station, it gives you a feeling of being part of the community. It will bring security and friendship and reduce inappropriate behaviors that attract the police, and crime will eventually reduce because of a police station that is around the corner, making it understandable to our young ones that the police are only doing their jobs. They are not enemies.

Building police stations in the suburbs will help normalize situations when one is being stopped or questioned by the police. It will feel normal, reducing the use of force or bad reaction from both sides if there is a stop by the police.

Neighborhood patrolling by the police will also help in avoiding police brutality because prevention is the key. Patrolling frequently by the police can also prevent burglary, robbery, auto theft, vandalism, shooting, kidnapping, and raping and other bad behaviors because when these criminals see the presence of police officers, they hide and are deterred.

Neighborhood patrolling needs to be expanded and improved. It will definitely make a calm community. When the mayor, council leaders, and police department have meetings, they might decide to pick a few people chosen by the mayor to keep an eye out or share information with the police.. They are not police; their job is to be the eyes and ears of the community. The police should join the meeting at least once a month or, as preferred by them, and do checks and balances on how the community is doing and if there is anything to amend or implement to help prevent crime before it hits. It is said, it is better to be careful than to be sorry. By paying these informants a couple of dollars, they can come up with a program based on lecturing people on how to behave appropriately and safely if stopped or approached by the police. It's not okay to use rude or swear words, like curse words or the F-word, when talking to the police.

Police are trained with force and equipped with force to perform their duties. Even if you have a weapon with you, like a gun, knife, Taser, or anything like that in your car, don't try to grab it, show it off, or use it. Continually teaching and reminding people about the basic things they should and shouldn't do when stopped by the police can make the relationship between the community and the police become more normal and successful.

Body cameras should be mandatory. There is a serious need for body cameras, security cameras, and license-plate readers. Put a security camera on roads. It will assist in dictating theft and footage, street fighting, and crackdown on drag racing. Police body cameras should be on at all times. Cameras can sometimes reveal helpful footage when trying to solve cases. Cameras, in general, can help police officers with audio and video, a person's face, and even license-plate information if they are needed. Police should patrol our inner cities to give us maximum peace, security, and order, though it can be challenging sometimes. That is the reason why cameras should be mandatory today. Police should always wear body cameras on duty to better improve job performance, quality, and efficiency. It will always be a reminder for them to bring home a good name for the police department because the police department who sent them to work is watching them like Santa, it sees when they do a good or bad job.

People should be truthful and respectful to the police because respect is reciprocal. Always drive with your driver's license and if you don't drive, always have some sort of ID on you. Every public housing apartment, church, school, college, university, hospital, restaurant, bar, supermarket, grocery store, and even park mandatorily should have cameras and metal detectors. Knowing that there is a camera can force somebody who wants to make a bad decision to change his/her mind because he/she knows that a camera is watching. Cameras can show when someone does something wrong. They can also help the police catch the person quickly before they do it again. Metal detectors are very important to these public buildings. Before people enter the door, the detector will do its job, thereby reducing the appearance of guns in such sensitive areas, saving lots of lives.

The police are capable of knowing anything about you, so be easy on them, and they will be easy on you, and they may even give you a verbal warning instead of a ticket, or instead of a punishment if you are hardheaded. Obedience goes a long way. When you hear a stop order by a police officer, please stop right away. Do not run away from the police, as it might generate the use of force and if you are not careful, it could turn into excessive force. Do not run over police with your car, because his coworkers may retaliate, which can be deadly.

IF THE POLICE HAPPEN TO BE THE ONES

If the police happen to be the ones who break the law, they will equally pay a fine or time or resign, they also could get fired for their crime of wrongdoing. Laws should be followed by all people and officers. It is essential for police officers to wear a body camera while they are doing their job. Cameras capture footage, noises, types of force applied regarding incidents or encounters, hit and run footage, locations, conditions, faces, and those that may be involved in any confrontation. Police body cameras should be worn at all times as long as they are on duty. Cameras should be activated before the start of any encounter, both audio and video. It should be high-tech and automatic so that there will be no room for excuses for what happened. If there is a need, possibly equip it with a look-back feature or an automatic camera so that cases can easily be disputed. Disciplinary actions should be required if not promptly followed by police officers.

Standardized policing is needed in our community. If, for any reason, an officer shoots an individual, they should call for medical assistance right away and try to give him/her CPR to help with the breathing or compression on the wound to help stop the bleeding. Encouraging words, that assistance is on the way, can be helpful. "You are going to be okay," is ideal because you are encouraging one to hang on to his/her life. It can really make one hopeful until assistance comes. This is not the time for any kind of disrespect. Imagine if it was you or someone in your house. Police should not use force or be rude or use abusive words and language. It is not acceptable anytime, especially at the time a human being is in a matter of life and death. They deserve comforting words, not physical and emotional pain due to what comes out of a police officer's mouth.

WHAT TO DO AND
WHAT NOT TO DO

There has been a fire drill in our schools for years to teach what to do and what not to do when there is a fire, and it has successfully saved lots of lives. Every month, firemen from the fire department will visit schools for a fire drill reiterating again what to do and what not to do if a fire breaks out. I strongly suggest that there be the same pattern for better policing in our communities and cities. Let there be once-a-month police drills, to teach in our schools, from pre-kindergarten to high school and colleges, at least the basic dos-and-don'ts drill when stopped by police or any interaction with police. Do not reach for any weapon. Do not flare or wave any weapon at the police. Do not point any weapon at the police. Do not use any weapon to threaten the police. Do not resist arrest. If the police tell you to stop, please stop right away. Do not bite the police.

It is good to greet the police or say thank

you for all they do. If you make it easy for the police, they will make it easier for you. Again, this is where first impressions matter. For us, it has been so long and confusing, not everyone knows or remembers what to do anymore, but this education and constant reminders will definitely save lives in both ways. School children and those in colleges will eventually take the message home to their brothers and sisters, parents, uncles, cousins, and friends. When they grow and start driving, going about their businesses in the community or their country, they will always remember what they learned.

Instead of carrying or showing weapons when dealing with the police, it's better to wear a calm demeanor and try to peacefully resolve the situation.. If for any reason you need to stay calm to avoid getting into trouble, when the police ask you a question, only answer it. Answer what you know, do not answer what you do not know It's important to only answer questions when you know the answer. Even if the police find an unlicensed gun in your possession, staying calm and not making up answers is the best way to handle the situation and avoid unnecessary trouble.

I also suggest flyers at motor vehicles and churches and supermarkets or grocery stores for basic right behavior, dos and don'ts, when stopped by a police officer for any reason as not everyone knows what to do in those situations. Some people were told by their parents, others did not receive the same lecture, and others have forgotten, especially people of color who have a history of overcoming a lot. It is a helpful reminder if the Dept. of Motor Vehicles would add onto their pamphlets or flyers good behavioral and safety tips with police while driving their vehicles. Educating the public on safe driving behaviors, benefits, and traffic laws, will help in the reduction of problems, mistreatment, or misrepresentation, and racial disparities people might experience with the law enforcement during a traffic stop or police encounter In the communities.

My brothers and sisters, a suggestion from my heart, when you are stopped by a police officer or have any encounter with them, please obey every instruction or order they give you from the first minute. This is where "obey before complain" will be applicable so that you will be on the same page with the government who sent them to work, but if they mistreat you in any way, the justice system will prevail for you. Don't intentionally bump into police officers with your car. We understand that accidents can occur, but please don't purposefully collide with a police officer on the road or at checkpoints. They're there to keep us safe. Do not create a situation where there has to be a car chase. If police said, put your hands up in the air, please put your hands up in the air right away. Do not flare or wave any weapon at police, for they are not mind readers and do not know what you are thinking at any moment. All they can go on is your actions so keep them in line with their instructions.

Do not throw any object at the police, for that might provoke and agitate them, forcing them to protect their own lives, and the reaction might be dangerous. Do not shoot police, for they will shoot back with more force. I have seen it time after time, many times, it has never worked for us. It always leads to death or permanent injury, especially of our black brothers, people of color, young people, even police too. Many lives have been lost, but we can fix this problem. With a change of attitude and way of response from both sides, we shall be safe and live happily again. Let us stop walking around ready for a fight.

IF WE ARE STOPPED BY THE POLICE, REMEMBER TO SAY, "YES, SIR" OR "YES, MA'AM" AND "NO, SIR" OR "NO, MA'AM" WHAT I AM PREACHING IS LIVE AND LET LIVE BETWEEN POLICE AND COMMUNITY. WHEN THE SPIRIT OF MISUNDERSTANDING COMES UP, THE SPIRIT OF UNDERSTANDING GOES AWAY.

BY CHANCE

By chance, if you ever have a gun on you or in your car, do not reach for it. Even if the police search you or your car and find a gun, since you did not shoot at them or try to reach for the gun, including any other type of weapon, police will not shoot you either, and lives will be saved. If the gun is registered in your name, you will still get it back. It makes more sense to lose money for a fine and give service for a time than to lose a whole precious life or remain seriously or permanently injured.

DURING HOLIDAYS

During holidays, Christmas for instance, people should visit police stations in their communities and tell them 'Thank you' for what they do for our communities. Buy them gifts or lunch. Make the police feel welcomed and appreciated. A little friendly visit like that will go a long way. It will not make matters worse; instead, it will help things run smoothly year after year, knowing that they were appreciated by the community they help to protect. Police, if possible, can do toy drives and give them to the children in the community, showing them at an early stage of their lives that the police are not enemies, rather can be friendly and are part of the community.

Statistically, blacks are mostly affected by this sudden death, brutality and misunderstanding. Our well-abled men and women and celebrities in the community should sometimes invite police offices to our parties, birthdays, open houses, engagement parties, and weddings. Give invitation cards to some men and women in uniform. Let us interact with them together, with or without uniform, sit closer, talk, eat, drink, have fun, laugh, and see each other's faces. Let us give them a ticket sometimes to go in their free time and relax somewhere, maybe with families or coworkers. By doing this, hopefully, it will bring among us friendship and a sense of belonging, a stronger and better community.

Our comedians should invite the police sometimes in their free time to come and listen to comedy so that we can laugh together. This will help people realize that they are human beings like us, they have feelings. The only difference is that they have a uniform with a "tool belt" on them. The community also needs to see the police without uniforms because for some, when they see police officers, they immediately feel uncomfortable or intimidated for some reason, so it will be helpful if people in the community see the police in uniform and also without uniforms, smiling and laughing. Seeing police officers without uniforms in their midst can help ease the tension making people feel more comfortable as well as give the police a better image within the community.

It is good if police officers maintain a friend and approachable demeaner while doing their job in the community. The look on a police officer's face can increase or decrease tension, whether while ticketing or questioning a person of interest. Police officers have nothing to lose by putting on a cool and friendly face on the job. Police should avoid the abuse of power but treat people with respect and dignity; especially when dealing with deceased individuals. Even when someone has passed away, they should be treated with care and respect.

Police, while doing their job, should approach a suspect or person in question with dignity, they should not have the impression of talking down to human beings and expect a respectful and better outcome. Somebody being poor or of a different race does not mean he/she deserves different treatment. Red, white, blue, black, or brown should not determine treatment. One way of handling people is not the only way to deal with people.

A suspect is not guilty until proven guilty.

Everyone should be treated equally. For example, a black professor or a retired black judge is out taking a stroll to get in a little exercise, and the police talk to him/her with no respect and detain him/her falsely. Eventually, he/she is found to be innocent. That will make it difficult for people of the same color, especially the young ones, not to resist arrest. They will think that, in one way or the other, no one is safe in the hands of the police. If an innocent suspect is treated like a person who committed a crime, but at the end, you realize that he/she is innocent after rough handling on land or in the car, that will also generate hate, distrust, and disrespect to police officers.

Abuse of power is the reason why some resist and flee whenever stopped by the police, which is dangerous. Sometimes, a wrongful arrest made by police should be concealed and cleaned up under an innocent individual's name.

Abstain yourself from abuse of any kind, and do not violate restraining orders because if violated, it can cause conflicts and fighting, which attracts law enforcement. There is a tendency that somebody who is already violent and acting agitated towards a private citizen can equally turn violence to police officers when they arrive, acting with the mind of misunderstanding. It can lead to a dangerously unexpected situation, ending in one permanently injured or dying. Moreover, when calls are made to get assistance from the police, you do not know what the caller told the police like if he/she told the police that the abuser is holding a gun or knife and is trying to kill him/her. It is certain that the police will be coming prepared, so it is better to be careful than to be sorry. Stop behaving like a bad citizen. This means not grabbing people; girls, women, boys, men, or homeless people- and insulting or assaulting, raping, punching, stabbing, slashing, pushing, or stealing from them. These ugly behaviors will attract the police's attention and draw necessary law and order.

Consider the way you dress, pull up your pants, buckle up your belt because you will look smart already or otherwise look suspicious already. Any hairstyle is acceptable, just trim, cut, and leave it clean. Talk like a good person; avoid starting to talk with curses to fellow citizens or police. It could be a police officer who intended to help for any reason; do not let cursing pass more than what you want or have to say, it could be provocative and triggering. Somebody watching by the side may call the police, and the police are the last people you want when you are already provoked. Walk gently like a gentleman/ gentlewoman, for the way you dress, not the amount you paid for the dress, the way you talk, and the way you walk can speak much about you already.

Again, avoid bad behavior or attitude that will attract unrest and the police, rioting, pushing people into an oncoming train, starting a fire, breaking and entering, slander, libel, battery, running a red light, avoiding traffic-light violation, for it can quickly turn fatal and brutal if it leads to a chase, pushing and beating elderly people, for it may not end up peacefully for you. Prevention is better than cure.

I'm calling on our celebrities. This is the time for big brothers and big sisters to talk. You can send a representative or virtual talk. Share some of the knowledge that you gained. Let your fellow citizens, in the urban, suburban, rural, in the community, know the truth that obedience, respect, loyalty, and forgiveness can go a long way with our struggle. Encourage basic dos and don'ts when having an encounter with a police officer. Tell them to listen and obey instructions from the police officer right away, and do not resist arrest. Remind them to do their best to make every encounter with the police end well, not end lives so they can make it home to their families. They will listen, and it will surely save lives.

I'm also calling on our religious groups and leaders of services, Christians, Muslims, Hindus, every denomination, priests, pastors, fathers, men and women of God, to do their part, to keep praying without ceasing for our country in general in the day and in the night and also for understanding between the police and the community. When your congregation is leaving, you want them to come back again, not missing one person. Let your congregation know when the sermon or mass is finished, and they are on their way going home, to remember to respect and obey men and women in uniform, to comply with any order given to them by the police officer, and to never bring out any weapon at all when stopped by the police. It is about saving souls and lives for God. Let us trade ego for our life to the fullest. Again, the first order you hear from the police- -for example, "Stop" please do stop the next minute. If you mistakenly have a gun on you, or a weapon of any kind, please drop the weapon immediately. If the police told you, put your two hands up in the air, immediately do what the police said.

You may call it courage, sacrifice, endurance, peacemaker, good citizen, stepping up to be the big guy, saving our own lives, but it is worth doing so that your life can be long in this beautiful land God has given us. By practicing these good behaviors, one will always go out there for his/her business and always come back home safe to his/her wife, husband, children, mom and dad, family, and friends. It breaks my heart to see people, especially blacks, whose young lives are cut short just because of a stop by the police. It is unbelievable, unacceptable, but fixable still. Let us turn this every other time occurrence around. It has to stop happening. We can fix it on our own. We cannot continue to ignore the violence in our community, too many gun-related deaths. Kids from as young as four years to teenagers to adults dying of gunshot wounds, stabbings, often it is from issues that could have been avoided. These guns and weapons are not killing somebody else. Instead, it is killing us, people-kids watching television in the parlor or in the room with siblings or a grandmother, children and adults celebrating birthday parties and having a barbecue.

IT IS HIGH TIME

It is high time to drop these guns or weapons and protect ourselves and our future. Our young people, remember to be loyal to your brothers and friends. Remember, the goodness between two people is extra contributed by one of them; you can be that person. In the book of Matthew, verse 26:52, Jesus said to Peter, "Put your sword in its place," you can call it a sword or gun or knife, "for those who live by the sword, die by the sword." One who uses violence can expect violence. It is better to try to use peaceful means whenever possible. There is another sword, a spiritual sword, that we are commanded in the scripture to use. Ephesians 6:17 says the sword of the scripture is the Word of God, the right sword. Street racing or drag racing, or speed contests on public roads, streets, and highways should be a thing of the past. Drag racing, oftentimes, leads to loss of lives, freedom, and time and money. The moment it is happening, it automatically turns our community into a dangerous and unhealthy zone because everybody is walking and running their businesses. People of all ages, taking a run or a stroll for exercise as well as mothers and babysitters pushing strollers should be safe on the road.

COSTING THE COMMUNITY THEIR FREEDOM

Drag racing is dangerous. It costs the community their freedom. They will be afraid of the danger that comes with racing. While over speeding costs lives in a time of accidents, people die, get seriously injured, or get permanently injured for no good reason. Any drag racing that catches the attention of police automatically ignites police chases, it could be on both land and air with helicopters. It is a waste of time and money the police should use to tackle other necessary assignments. Police can die or seriously get hurt while performing this unnecessary task. When cars collide, depending on what they collided with, it costs money for both vehicles to get repaired, or they may damage government properties, thereby causing taxpayers to waste money for all the repair of the damaged properties.

The sniping of police officers should stop. Women and men of the police force have families like us. They feel pain; and of course, some policemen and policewomen have died due to anger from people, perhaps for what has happened in the past or during a current event. But they happen to be good police. Sometimes, while attending to a 911 call, they will be sniped down. That also is not acceptable and should stop. They have wives, husbands, children, parents, family, and friends. The police have good intentions for us. They go the extra mile to serve the community. They protect.

Imagine if you have a conflict with a person whose chest is ten times bigger than yours, who are you going to call? It is the police. The police protect us during good and bad weather, storms, hurricanes, and pandemics day and night. They rescue us and our pets from burning buildings and cars. The police deliver babies on the highway where hospitals and doctors and nurses are not yet available. They keep us safe on the road, if we miss the road or get lost in the woods, the police will even go so far as to help by walking with a person with dementia until he/she is safe in the hands of his/her family member.

Gun violence, excessive gun activities in our communities like robbery and shootings contributes to police brutality. Any criminal act attracts the police because it is their duty to do a lot of jobs, including enforcement of law and order and security can easily cause police brutality. Gun violence also affects our communities because all these bullet-related deaths are almost due to gun violence. Citizens endure violent crimes in our communities going to school, going to bus stops, to restaurants, to the park, during a walk in the neighborhood, driving their car in the communities, going to games, even while getting a car wash. Because of these excessive shootings, even in the heart of the communities, the country is losing its economy due to tourists no longer wanting to visit the United States. They fear for their lives, and others run away from their businesses, even if America still has other wonderful and beautiful people and places.

WE CAN CHANGE ANYTHING WE PUT OUR MINDS TO.

POLICE SHOULD DO EVERYTHING IN THEIR POWER

Police should do everything in their power to avoid searching wrong homes and leaving these innocent people with insults and bad memories for the rest of their lives. When searches such as this are done in error, a serious warning or a fine should be given to the police officers as a consequence. It is a serious violation of human rights and privacy, and you will hardly convince these individuals again that the police are there to protect them.

Another thing, police should be cautious about the way of knocking at the resident's door or home when they have a warrant that requires visiting the suspect's home. Some people call it "home." Others call it "house." Home is where people have privacy, where they rest or sleep, wear dresses or not, and raise their children, so have respect. A knock that is too loud at the door can agitate a homeowner. The way police knock at somebody's house can lead to a difficult and disturbing assignment or can lead or help to a successful visit and job well done. Police should not knock anxiety, agitation, and fear into people before they even see the police uniform. It is okay to knock nicely, saying the reason for visiting. Everybody is different. Too loud of a noise can cause somebody sleeping on the couch to go back in the house and get a weapon before opening the door, which may not be friendly anymore, causing homeowners or police to get hurt. It can even be deadly to innocent residents or neighbors. Police officers should give them a little time also, maybe they have to put on clothing. A polite knock on the door can lead to a safe and successful job done by the police.

Having a good understanding is very important for both people and the police; it should be applied whenever there is an encounter between them. Police departments should do more in retraining police officers in different areas, including information gathering, to avoid knocking on wrong doors that have been rising lately, killing, and wrongful arrest of innocent homeowners or residents. People in the community should understand that what matters is doing every discipline you can to make it home to your family as a final result.

Language matters. Police should use language they will understand. They should talk to people and let them know that they matter. If people are resisting arrest or refusing to drop their weapon when instructed, police should let them know that they do not want to get hurt and that their lives matter. It may touch their heart that they matter and may lead them to put down the weapon. Police should not shoot anyone who drops their weapon. That should be against the law.

STAY HOME IF NECESSARY

Stay home if necessary- -home sweet home. Home is where love is. This is to avoid some of the trouble out there. It could be arguing or fighting with a friend or stranger. It could be getting hit by a car or a stray bullet. You could cut up with a drug abuser or stay at the right place at the wrong time. Most of the time, it is safe at grandmother's house or aunty's house. No matter how old you are, it is always warm and welcoming at grandma's house. They would like to see you every day rather than not at all.

Music is therapeutic. Choose any music that suits you at the moment. Enjoy and save your day and also save your life. Stay home, watch your favorite shows, or play games. Maybe from today, just make out a day in a week, or month, to stay home no matter what. Sometimes, staying home is equal to staying out of trouble out there. When one stays home, there is the possibility of avoiding gunshots or police brutality or any kind of brutality out there.

Go to bed early, for early to bed is early to rise. The world has changed so much that staying out there from two to three o clock in the morning and not doing much is not important or worth it. Until the world changes back to the old good way, staying home if possible can prevent staying at the right place at the wrong time, which may mean danger. There is no place like home, they said. People have favorite spots in their homes that they enjoy more than others, even though they might not use some areas.

Cook and eat if you can, order food and beverages if you can or drink water. Get fresh air on the front porch, enjoy a good shower or enjoy your Jacuzzi if you have one. Enjoy your bed, get rest, relax in your parlor, watch boxing, or sports. There are so many things you can enjoy in your own house to avoid all the trouble out there.

Love thy neighbor as yourself, the Bible said. While we are taking guns out of the wrong hands, put love in. Love is another necessary pillar that holds together the police and the community. Only love can bring out the best of the police and the community they serve. Love is the only pillar that can hold the whole world together.

The community should do its part also to avoid police brutality. They should practice love and human rights, not hate and racism. Recognize that everyone in the community deserves their right to be loved unconditionally and have respect for each other by avoiding hate crime and racism. There is no need to physically or emotionally hurt one another. Racism and hate cause a lot of harm in the society, like excluding someone from stores or restaurants, leaving hurtful messages on cups or receipts, making negative gestures, using offensive language, and unfairly arresting people solely based on their skin color, race, or gender. Racism and hate cause a lot of harm in society.

People in the community must say no and stand up for what is right. Love is very important in everything we do in life, choosing best friends, marriage, or choosing an occupation or job. When there is love, there is less room for brutality between the police and the community. The police and the people in the community can work well together by giving each other a little agape love, the kind of love God has for us. For a police officer to truly effective in his/her job, he/she must love to be a police officer. Police jobs are quite challenging, but with love, come rain or sun, one will go to work and do their job to their best ability and will try to avoid anything that will demote their performance but instead embrace love, tolerance, and respect. When a police officer loves his job, he/she is also happy and also will love people in the community he/she serves.

When Jesus was teaching in parables, there was, "Love thy God with all your heart," and "Love thy neighbor as yourself." Who is your neighbor? A man was going from Jerusalem to Jericho. The road from Jerusalem to Jericho was hot and dry. It was rough and dangerous. He was robbed, beaten, and left to die. Many people passed him by for example: a priest, Levite, Samaritan- and did nothing to help, but because of the love of God, a Good Samaritan, a person who was not expected to help him is the one who helped him get up and paid for his wound to be bound and treated. I believe the majority of policemen and policewomen are good. They run toward danger to save lives while everyone else will be running away from danger. They answer some calls and even come back in a couple of minutes with food. Some practice love by making a payment using their own money for a shoplifter instead of making an arrest.

The people in the community should not see the police as enemies, but instead as friends and neighbors. To help avoid brutality, the police should continue to show more love to the community they serve. They can give verbal or written instructions or warnings instead of tickets. The police should give extra seconds or minutes to allow a peaceful surrender when having any encounter while working in the community. The people in the community should practice giving love back by respecting and responding to the police officer in a timely manner.

If you apply love, do not be surprised when a person you think is your enemy might turn out to be the only one to help you when other people have run away or when you are in need. Loving your neighbor has nothing to do with being near or close in place or time but the opportunity to do good for somebody who is in need in one way or the other. Love is caring and protecting each other in the community. Instead of pulling the trigger, change your mind not to pull the trigger because it can cause a police officer, someone in the community, or even a child to get hurt or worse.

Love is not engaging in anything that will cause trouble. Love for our community is seeing something and saying something. Love is when a police officer imagines themselves in the shoes of a person they're dealing with and treats them how they'd want their own family member to be treated in the same situation. Who is your neighbor? Anybody who lives within your community is your neighbor. It could be policemen or policewomen, officers, firefighters, military personnel, healthcare workers, lawmakers at Capitol Hill, lawyers, teachers, students, autistic children, or the disabled. Look out for your neighbors. Do not leave your autistic neighbor to wander away on your watch. It is time for us to go back to practicing being good neighbors. Do not abandon or ignore your neighbor because he/she is a police officer or because he/she is your enemy or because of their skin color, gender, or ethnicity. Talk to them, hear them out, and respect and help them if help is needed. Do it for God, and you will not regret doing it.

Relating to our neighbors will help in avoiding any kind of brutality, including police brutality. Racism and inequality are other big factors in fighting police brutality. Racism has to go for the police and the people in the community to trust each other. It is said that a happy wife makes a happy home. Likewise, happy people and police make a happy community. Where equality is practiced, makes happy policing. We need equality in our schools in the buildings we frequent, and in workplaces. People in the community are not supposed to practice or experience racism and inequality.

The division of this people or group is white, black, Latino, Asian, gay, lesbian. A certain group of people may have more power or privilege that allows them to get away with certain things while others cannot due to the way they are received and seen by others. That is practicing racism and inequality. We were created equal by the Creator of the universe. This kind of behavior is not acceptable. It can equally bring anger, discomfort, people not listening to each other, even the police officers, due to the treatment they have received from a particular group or race. Inequality and maltreatment that comes with it can lead to people moving from their community or city to another, or from one country to another country, where there is no practice of inequality or racism. The villagers, communities, everyone, will try their best to fight and stop inequality and racism because it will always be the final product of instability and brutality, causing stress to humanity like moving from one place to another, or one country to another country.

The stress and heartbreak that comes from inequality and racism and fear, in general, and not having the sense of belonging in their so-called community where some races are few and inferior, among others, can be overwhelming. Some people are attacked, pushed to the ground, both young and elderly, killed, called names, and followed. Some, when they walk in certain areas or wear a certain dress, the police will be called on them. For some races, if they were seen walking in a certain number, the police will be called on them, even if they are not damaging anything. It's even to the point where some individuals cannot attend nice schools in their community or zip code due to their race.

INEQUALITY AND RACISM ARE REAL

Inequality and racism are real. An African American driving an expensive car is likely to be stopped by the police than a lesser-valued car and can get questioned if he/she is in a neighborhood where they feel they don't belong; This does not happen to their white counterpart. In many cases, blacks are more than likely to be pulled over while driving than whites. You will detest it if you are on the other side, and it must be tackled. It can never bring any value to the well-being of humanity, when people cannot accept and listen to one another or treat others like themselves because of what they look like or their beliefs. These kinds of behaviors can cause brutality, including police brutality.

Carjacking, when there is a lack of job opportunities, people, youths, easily get distracted. Since everybody behaves differently, some will choose to steal, shoplift, or carjack. To avoid police brutality, do not carjack or do any of the things I listed. The minute the owner of the car notifies the police that their car is missing, with the information, the police will be on their way to hunt down the carjackers. Many times, it involves speeding from both police and carjackers because a carjacker is driving to get away from the police officer, and the police are chasing them to recover the car. Sometimes, it ends up causing an accident for both parties, the police and the individual, or one party. It can be brutal sometimes if the carjacker decides not to surrender to the police. Carjacking can cause innocent bystanders to get hurt. Sometimes, they shoot at the police, which can contribute to exchanging gunshots and bullets, which makes the situation worse and potentially fatal.

TO AVOID POLICE BRUTALITY

To avoid police brutality, police officers should avoid police fatigue. They should not overwork themselves, working around the clock without rest. They should take shifts because policing is one of the most stressful and tiring jobs. They need to be on point at all times. Police officers should not come to work drunk and intoxicated. Police officers should not lose their tempers on duty, for anger and impatience could worsen the situation with any encounter. They should not sleep at work to make sure they are alert at all times.

Knowing that everybody has a boss, the police should do their job professionally in order to give a good account at the end of the day, which, in the long run, will earn him or her recognition and a pay raise in connection with a happy workplace and loving what you do. Police officers should arrive at work on time to avoid being disorganized at the beginning of the shift, which may affect their whole day at work. Police officers should call out in a timely manner, enough time for their colleagues to arrange for another officer to come in if he/she cannot come into work because fewer workers mean less production. They deserve a good amount of time for vacation and breaks, in order to de-stress, cool their eyes and brain, eat food if they are hungry, and get refreshed to go back for the remaining hours strong and fit.

Police officers should show respect to fellow officers and all people at all times. The police should always be ethical, doing the right thing with their profession and acting with good intentions, not being unethical such as using lethal or excessive force on people in the community during any encounter, or pulling someone out of a car by his/her hair during a traffic stop. Illegal search and seizure of items from the people in the community, accepting bribes or unauthorized gifts, false arrest or detention of the citizens, these kinds of behaviors can violate the police work ethic and cost them some respect from the community they serve. It can lead to brutality when respect is lacking from both police and people.

Give police officers a pay raise, for everybody likes a pay raise. They will be appreciative and be happier at work and do everything in their power to keep their job. Sometimes, salary is motivating. A worker is more likely to perform to his/her potential if he/she is happy with the salary he/she is earning, and police officers are no different. A police officer well paid feels valued by his management. They say to whom much is given, much is expected, and they will do everything they can to impress the management that sent them to work with their professionalism. But a police officer who is paid less for the amount of work they do may be angry without complaining, and that anger will affect the people in the community in the form of brutality. Police not well-paid can contribute to many leaving the workforce, making it stressful for a reduced number of workers. Less productivity due to lack of enough workers, and the community will reap the end product of the police not having enough workers.

Police reform should happen now to avoid the continuation of mistaken deaths of the people in the communities, especially those from communities of color, who are hurt or killed by police officers due to excessive force in the form of chokeholds, kneeling on someone's neck, or shooting innocent people in their homes by mistake.. They should find a way to de-escalate safely with no injury or death involved.

THINK

To avoid police brutality, do not take police officers possessions, for example, police cars or officers' guns. If you take an officer's gun from him, they will assume you are automatically armed and mean harm to them so you will be met with police brutality. You can seriously get hurt from doing that act. Even if you do not want to shoot the police officer, you took the gun so that the police will not shoot you, but the other officers, remember, will not be able to read your mind. Therefore, leave the officers' possessions alone. If someone gets away with a police car or gun, the police will not rest until they locate the person because the police will think that the person is dangerous to himself, other people, or to the police officers.

AS A GOOD CITIZEN

As a good citizen, people should not go behind the wheel drunk, for that will impair your driving. You or someone else can get hurt, and you can cause an accident. Driving drunk violates government law. Innocent people can lose their lives if one causes an accident due to overdrinking. Having a blood alcohol level above the legal limit can land one in jail and cause them to be faced with a huge fine. It attracts police attention when somebody is driving impaired. It can be brutal because a drunk might be able to think clearly or control themselves. It would be advisable to let someone else drive you home. For a whole lot of good reasons, if you get home safe, so does everyone else. As an alternative, you can page car services that will take you home. It is a very good idea for someone else to be the driver, not the one who is drunk.

Avoid engagements and activities that are gang-related, for that can quickly put one into police brutality.

Remember always, when a firefighter engine or truck, siren ambulance, or police siren car is on the road, you must clear away from the road. People in the community, whether you are walking, bicycling, motorcycling, or driving, must always remember to clear out of the road because it could be a matter of life and death for somebody who is sick. It could be someone who had an accident that needs emergency medical attention, or it could be a building burning down, it could be an accident that police is rushing from to save a life where they secure the road and escort a car or an ambulance to the hospital, that kind of assignment cannot be interrupted, or it can be fatal. People should, at all times, always wait for them to pass.

JOB OPPORTUNITIES AND HEAVY INVESTMENTS

Job opportunities and heavy investments in black communities will cut the effect of police brutality in more than half. Investments like jobs, free education, equality or inclusivity, end racism and push for respect and security. An idle mind is a devil's workshop. In order to help fight police brutality, there has to be job opportunities. The government should create jobs from the federal to the states and importantly in the local governments, cities, communities for people to be employed, keep busy, and make money to help with their everyday needs. Having people in the community working can prevent them from stealing and give them a reason to stay away from trouble. Maybe city jobs, private-sector training jobs, and the government should also help people who want to be self-employed. They said money is the root of all evil. People working and earning their own money will help a lot in reducing those evil crimes that lead to killing people, damaging properties (even ones that belong to the government), and robbing banks or gas stations.

All these young and beautiful people, their blood is still pumping hot and hard and they're full of energy. You have to keep them busy with good-paying jobs because if you do not keep them busy in a good way, they are going to be busy in a bad way. In order to keep the youths safe, out of trouble and to stay at home, at their working place, or in school, the employers may consider adding extra hours and extra money or bonus pay during the summertime. This will give people an incentive to work, instead of loitering about making trouble that can land them in the hands of police. The federal and local government should help the business in the cities with a summer allocation.

The government also funding amusement parks or places of fun will help so that a lot of people can afford it and also keep themselves busy in a good way, also giving free education and bonus money for people who will attend summer schools. A longer school year, which is summer school, is worth exploring as a way to close the achievement gap, raise test scores for lower-income students, and keep young minds engaged and productive. Schools across America should follow the idea of supporting and giving bonuses for summer schools effective immediately because attending summer school helps one to graduate early and get a job in time to take care of oneself. The safety of the future, greatness and glory of our nation partially depends on it, keeping the youths active in a good way and dedicated.

Federal, state, and local governments should build and sponsor music theaters or booths, where young ones can have another way to keep themselves busy in a good way, learn how to sing, how to play piano, instead of cursing and bearing the consequences from trouble. The government can also help by building free sports centers to keep youths away from loitering about and away from trouble. They can practice and play, for example, soccer, basketball, football, track and field, or learn how to wrestle or box to also reduce the energy that puts them in trouble sometimes. These kinds of ideas can bring out the best of them, world-class musicians and athletes as our representatives of tomorrow on the world stage and also reduce police brutality in our communities, because if the youths are not at home resting, they are in school learning, if they are not at their jobs, making money, if they are at the amusement park having fun, if they are not at the music theater learning music, then they are at the sport center, boxing.

IF SOMEONE GETS INVOLVED

If someone gets involved in drug or human trafficking, they are absolutely calling for police brutality because a police officer cannot watch drug dealers smuggle drugs and human beings into our society. That will easily destabilize and destroy our children because some people can use drugs knowingly, but others can accidentally use it without knowing. Some of our educated ones are now disorganized with drug addiction. Some cannot finish college, due to addiction. Some are walking on our streets, thinking they are still what they used to be. And eventually, they are not themselves anymore and so many other bad reasons due to the effect of drugs. Some emptied their savings.

When someone who uses drugs started to act differently and not in their usual way, that is a big health issue that is going to take a long time to correct, sometimes, never corrected again, which is called addiction. The addiction affects the person and his/her family members, friends, neighbors, and coworkers. All these bad behaviors, such as stealing, killing, drug trafficking, human trafficking, gun trafficking, in society can affect the court system by giving them too many cases on criminal matters. It also costs the government huge amounts in terms of money for investigation, housing, deportation, treatment, and rehabilitation.

The police do not play with drug matters because drugs are the killer of a nation especially the young ones, to avoid police brutality or one spending the rest or half of their lifetime behind bars, instead depend on one's pocket and hustle with selling cold beverages, water and certain snacks. God works in mysterious ways; you never know who is watching and decides to help and one will be happy instead of getting in big trouble.

AVOIDING POLICE BRUTALITY SHOULD START AT HOME

Avoiding police brutality should start at home. Parents have to teach their children law and order. It is said that charity begins at home, while Proverbs 22:6 in the Bible said, "Train up a child in the way he should go, and even when he is old he will not depart from it." Parents, teach your children to obey before complaining when a police officer stops them for any reason and to kindly listen and follow his/her instructions or orders so that he/she would be able to avoid any type of conflict that will lead to brutality. As a parent, when you talk about police officers in front of your kids, be sure to highlight that the police are here to keep us safe and that they are not our enemies. As a parent, when stopped by the police, please compose yourself because kids are watching closely at everything you do, they learn from what they see or hear, and talk to police officers in a good manner because they will do the same when it is their turn.

It is important that parents rise up and help to stop this problem of brutality. Parents should advise their children to respect and obey the police in a timely manner. Let your children know that policemen and policewomen in their uniforms performing their jobs deserve our respect, not insults, and they should listen to them and do everything they ask right away because it is said that delay is dangerous. Delaying to comply with the police can only make the matter worse. I have seen it many times in the news on television, not making split-second compliance with the police has been working against us, so I strongly suggest that to make any encounter or a stop by the police end quickly and safely, one has to comply with the police in a timely manner. Not listening to police officers' instructions, commands, orders, and words can make the police feel disrespected, agitated, and insulted. It will look like a partial resistance, which may escalate things in the wrong direction against anyone who is not complying; therefore, the faster, the better. The faster and more calmly you comply with the police, the better, the safer, and the faster they let you go to do your business, or the faster they give you get the all clear. Not listening and complying in a timely manner may lead to mistakes, by police officers making mistakes against one's life.

A police officer can mistakenly grab a gun instead of a Taser, even if it is unprofessional to do that, but when a life is lost, it is forever. You can no longer take it back and do things differently, so the quicker one complies, the sooner one goes home safely with his life still full of potential. When stopped by the police, let them know that it is a time to stay calm and respectful and comply, not a time to talk back to a police officer, fight, or resist arrest, and it is not a time for knife-wielding or reaching for a gun. Do not knowingly accelerate your car towards an officer or officers. To avoid unfortunate loss of life, please comply with the police officer's first instruction.

Parents encourage your children to avoid the police, but do not leave or run away from the police while they stop you and are still talking to you. Rather, exercise patience. You can avoid the police by not breaking the law, not breaking traffic rules, like running a red light and exceeding the mileage needed on the road, by not stabbing people out there, not wielding weapons on police and other people, not burning down churches, synagogues, or mosques, for the buildings do not cause trouble, only people do. You can avoid the police by doing the right thing. But by chance, if you fail to maintain, and eventually, you are stopped by the police, allow them to ask questions, and make sure you are all cleared by the police before you leave to be on the safe side and to avoid any inconveniences because if you leave without being cleared by the police officer who stopped you, he/she may assume you are running away from him/her and may retaliate in a dangerous way.

Teachers also can help to stop police brutality by teaching these kids law and order at an early stage. They can make the kids follow the school laws, in other words, school rules, with no exception. This way, they can generate students who can obey the rules, law, and order now and tomorrow. Teachers can teach our kids to be color-blind at an early stage so that when they grow up, they will see everybody as the same, not skin color or ethnicity or what one looks like. Teachers should help by teaching pure history. We can learn from what happened before us to keep doing the good ones and reject bad ideas, treatments, mistreatments, and misrepresentations that happened in the past, that is the reason for pure history.

Teachers should not use the advantage of history to teach racism and hate. That is not acceptable. Not teaching pure history may fire up racism and hate, which may contribute to police brutality. Our children are supposed to learn that we all belong here together, regardless the skin color, race, ethnicity, back-ground, gender, profession, and religion, not teaching or encouraging repetition of what happened before making citizens turn against each other. We salute teachers who teach pure history and make good impacts in our children's lives.

Workplaces and gym management can also help spread the gospel about the importance of law and order to avoid police brutality. They can paste information about the basic things to do when stopped by the police in their offices, break rooms, waiting rooms, and hallways; and that surely will help generate a positive impact in our communities.

Politicians and political parties have to play a huge part in avoiding police brutality. When they are campaigning, they should apply and preach law and order. It does not matter which party one belongs to, it does not matter if it is going to favor them politically. It is their obligation to use their platforms to talk to people at the same time they are campaigning to be good citizens and respect and obey law and order, which means that one should always obey the law of the land. When they settle in power with lawmakers, they can make a law that certified gun owners who use their guns recklessly or do not protect guns against kids or teenagers, juveniles, or anybody who should have guns, should lose their right to have a gun for a long time or be fined heavily. This is because kids or any of these bodies can accidentally shoot themselves or others, even their parents, or point, wave, or shoot at the police, which, if it happens to the police, may end up brutal.

The political parties should help in telling the crowd the truth about law and order, not playing politics or lying for political gains.

TRAINING

Police dogs help in locating missing and endangered children and adults, even those missing in disasters like storms and hurricanes. Training more police dogs, K9, will help reduce fatality shootings. The K9 will somehow serve as the preparer of setting crooked places straight before the police officers. People are dog-friendly, no matter, regular or police dogs. Police dogs going first before police officers should possibly reduce fatality, which works hand in hand with brutality. For instance, if there is a drug presence, police going in first may cause a sudden shoot-out between police officers and people so it might be better of the police dog checks things out first to avoid a dangers shootout.

Police officers should call out their colleague who is not following their work ethic and is also using excessive or lethal force on the people in the community they serve. If a police officer is using excessive force on an individual, other police officers have to intervene; otherwise, the individual can get seriously hurt or die. Police officers should be held accountable if they watch and allow injustice to reign. They should pay a heavy fine for allowing that to happen. It will be helpful if the police federalize one style of executing their job. For instance, whatever is used for excessive force in one city or state and is bad, it should be the same across the nation. If kneeling on the neck or a choke hold or any restraining procedure is unlawful in one city or state, it should be the same across the nation in order to do their job professionally, and also, for people to know exactly what to do when they have encounter with the police. Standard or universal work ethic for the police department will help reduce police brutality.

De-escalation training tactics will also generate a huge amount of success in fighting police brutality. Police officers here and around the world should embrace the use of de-escalation instead of using force right away, beating sticks, guns as the first move, pushing to the ground, and beating with a stick or gun. First impressions can turn a peaceful person into resisting any order from the police, which can fuel police brutality.

MENTAL HEALTH CARE AND TREATMENT

Mental health care and treatment, it is high time the government recognize mental health problems as a public health problem. It affects a whole lot of people in the community, the mentally ill, the police, and the people around. It contributes to police brutality. When an individual is waving a knife or gun or pointing a gun at the police officer, the officer is not a mind reader to know that he/she is not well. The police officer may be agitated and react to ensure their safety, which may turn deadly, without knowing that the person waving the gun is very mentally ill. Whom is the government going to blame? A very mentally ill person or the police who wants to protect his/her life in the line of duty? It will reasonably help reduce police brutality if the government will care enough to provide mental health-care facilities and treatment for people who need it. A lot of threatening activities will reduce out there in our communities, which affects and attracts the police officers. When a mother or a family member cares enough to alert the police or government about a son, daughter, husband, or wife with threatening or suspicious behavior or who is making an alarming statement of being suicidal, shooting, or killing, that person should be looked into very seriously and given a mental health wellness check. The police or authority will no longer stop by asking for identifications and asking questions only but also kindly offer mental health wellness checks to the person concerned. If possible, the person will get checked. If there is a mental problem, he/she will get the care and treatment needed from the government. That act can save the individual, the police, and the people in the community. Also, it will reduce police brutality.

Homelessness goes hand in hand with mental health. A homeless man is equal to a hungry man. My people said that a hungry man does not sing hallelujah. A hungry man is an angry man. Sometimes, encounters between the police and the homeless don't end well because the police officers, might not know the status of the individual at the beginning and it turn brutal or deadly. The government should come to the aid of these police officers, the communities that are so dirty and filthy, and the homeless as well. These individuals did not choose to be homeless, it is time and change, sickness, or this life that goes ups and downs, and neither did they choose to be bad to the police officers. It is very important that the government pays urgent attention to this pressing matter, homelessness, or it is not going to go anywhere. However, if the government does intervene urgently, it will save lives, help police departments with their job, reduce brutality, and also stop the attacks and killing that goes with homelessness.

Arson burns down anything. Police officers can also help by exercising more patience with people in the communities because, at times, you do not know who is going through a lot. A homeless person attacks the police and people in the communities. For example, when a homeless person attacks somebody who is minding his/her business, police will not stay back, they will jump into action. Assume the homeless person stabbed a victim, and when police came, the homeless person still possessed the knife and attempted to stab the police officer and refuse to listen to drop the knife, which is threatening to the police, the homeless man's behavior can cause police brutality.

Again, charity begins at home. the United States of America is the most charitable country in the whole wide world. America spends billions of dollars on aid to other countries every year, which is a good thing to share, to render help with their well-being, but we forget about ourselves. Some of these people from other countries do not believe their eyes when they visit America and the rate of homelessness that exists on our streets in this country. It is time for America to start helping itself also by tackling homelessness and the tragedies that come with it.

Now is the time for the United States of America to use its taxpayers' money and take care of its people, including homeless people. I guarantee you; it will help reduce police brutality by three quarters. Give the homeless a home, it will mean peace for them, and assign them social workers to help track, care, and account for them until they are well abled again. If it is properly done and they are cared for, a homeless person can bounce back again. It is time for America to begin this aid and charity from home. Surely, it will be a big relief for people in the communities, police forces, and the country in general.

Life can be somehow slippery sometimes; life can change for good or bad in the blink of eye. It will make a good gesture for the government and people to care for the homeless, create jobs, and hire the homeless. Some of the homeless are educated with degrees; they just need a little help to get back on their feet again. Some are talented, like plumbers, electricians, painters, builders, guitarists, and singers.

The government should also lower mortgages and rents in America so that they are more affordable for people. This will also help to prevent people from going homeless.

Good gestures and looking out for each other can help reduce police brutality in the community. When you see a former neighbor, former friend, classmate, or stranger, do not pass him or her by; a smile or a kind hello can go a long way. When you see someone, ask how they are doing? If you see someone in need, offer money, food, job, clothing, anything that can help; it will truly go a long way.

MERCY WORK

Have we forgotten the work of mercy? The Lord encouraged us to do mercy work, in the world, teaching from the Bible. The work of mercy is giving drink to the thirsty, visiting the sick and burying the dead, comforting those in prison, feeding the hungry, clothing the naked, consoling the sorrow and sheltering the homeless. Offer shelter or an apartment if you can afford it. That will help in reducing the number of homeless people out there, for some people said that man is God to man, which sometimes appears to be truth. While others said that Jesus is going around doing favors.

One of the beatitudes says blessed are the merciful for they will be shown mercy or obtain mercy, and indeed surely good and mercy shall follow you all the days of your life if you cared from the heart. Matt5:7 says I am confident that a time will come for each of us when, whether because of sickness or infirmity, poverty or distress, of oppressive measures against us by man or nature, we shall wish for mercy.

REDUCING HOMELESSNESS

Reducing homelessness can help to reduce police brutality. Forgive and forget. Forgiveness is going to play a huge part in reducing police brutality. In the past and now, some people, some races, some color, felt mistreated or misrepresented by others, but it is time to let the old things go and a time for a new beginning, like a broken marriage that is fixed, and it becomes happy again. Husband and wife live in peace due to forgiveness. Sisters and brothers, friends, and friends live in peace due to forgiveness. It will surely make broken places straight again. If there is no sin or trespass, there will be no need for forgiveness. A police officer who is holding a grudge on a particular race or skin color is not going to execute a good profession. At the same time, a person of color or a particular race may not listen to the police officer he/she is holding a grudge against. That will make any encounter or a stop by the police difficult. That is enough reason for us to let forgiveness reign and play a role in the communities. If all of us will apply a little forgiveness, if we can be kind to each other and to ourselves, our world will be more loving and caring, and we will live in harmony.

HOLDING POLIC OFFICERS ACCOUNTABLE

The police department should look into holding police officers accountable or big punishments for police aiding and abetting criminals and criminal activities on duty. When police officers take an oath for their job, they promise to do their job to their best of their ability to serve and protect the community, but they refuse to carry it out, especially when it includes that of citizens dying in their hands against their wills.

"See something, say something" is not only for the citizens but also for police officers.

Police who are working together should also hold themselves and one another accountable when they see things are being done the wrong way. During an encounter, no police officer should walk into any situation with the intent to kill someone. Likewise, other police officers should not let one of their own kill somebody who is not supposed to die on their watch. If they let one of their own do that, then it means they are aiding and abetting, and all of them on duty at that moment should pay a fine in one way or the other. A very serious example of this aiding and abetting is what happened in Minneapolis, Minnesota, United States, on May 25, 2020, a day an African American man was murdered by a white police officer who works with the Minneapolis Police Department during an arrest or encounter after a store clerk alleged that he had passed a counterfeit twenty-dollar bill. One of the four police officers who arrived on the scene knelt on the neck of the African American man for nine minutes and twenty-nine seconds after he was handcuffed and lying face down on the ground. The black man should have been alive today and paid the consequences of his action, pay his fine for the crime he committed, but instead, he lost his life untimely because the other three police officers did not act fast, they did not intervene, instead, they watch the man die before their eyes. Their action of aiding and abetting contributed to his death and also their inaction landed them in trouble and their colleague in the biggest trouble. The white police officer was convicted of second-degree murder and manslaughter.

GUNS HAVE TURNED INTO TOYS IN OUR COMMUNITIES

Guns have turned into toys in our communities, so parents should know the kind of toys they buy for their children. Before teenage age, their minds have fallen in love with guns, whether toy guns or real guns. Children do not know the exact power and purpose of a gun. Nobody is supposed to use a gun or any weapon without knowing the proper use of it. This has caused a lot of tragedies in our communities, children shooting children and other people not knowing the differences and purposes of toy and real guns, not knowing it can hurt or kill them or anybody or lead to police brutality. For example, whether a nine-year-old or a nineteen-year-old is pointing a gun at the police officer, it will not always be easy to tell right away if it is a fake or a real gun; and it can be dangerous.

Even if the child is innocent, he/she does not know one cannot use a toy gun or real gun pointing at the police officer because she has been playing with something of that nature. In my opinion, parents should embrace other inspirational toys instead of introducing pure innocent minds to a toy that represents danger. Instead of children playing with toy guns, it is healthier to play hide-and-seek games like hopscotch, examples of good toys that teach caring, engineering, architecture, and cooking. When they are age appropriate and mentally healthy, they can exercise their right to bear arms and learn how to properly use a gun.

If they go to a military school, they will learn how to use guns, including military-style guns, so there is no need of introducing these innocent minds to guns early. Also, parents and caretakers should be watchful for the choice of video games and movies they and their children watch. They should know what their children are watching or playing and make sure it is not associated with dangerous actions and practices like pointing, wielding, and shooting guns and bombings. Some of these dangerous action movies have somehow motivated some kids, teenagers, and adults to practice what they watch. Sometimes, all these senseless killings and lives wasted are due to what they have been watching in the movies and playing on video games.

FIGHTING POLICE BRUTALITY IS GOING TO TAKE COLLABORATION

As I mentioned earlier, fighting police brutality is going to take collaboration between the community and the police. The people will try their best to do their part, but the police also have to contribute strongly to the success of this effort. Police have to acknowledge that there has been maltreatment and misrepresentation in the past, and it is still ongoing from fewer people for particular skin color or colors. For example, in Tulsa, Oklahoma, on May 31 and June 1, 1921, the massacre of Black Wall Street happened, a situation where white mobs looted and burned down the black district of Greenwood over an allegation that a black man had assaulted a white woman, which led to the deaths of black people. It could have also been treated differently than what happened.

A July 1967 riot in Newark, New Jersey; the riot was a race riot where white police officers treated blacks with no dignity and murdered them as if they were formidable living things as if their lives didn't matter. Both adults and young children felt mistreatment by the police. History has carried it. Ancestors told their children and children's children, which made their generations believe that white police officers, but not all white police, were meant to brutalize them till today. Therefore, police officers in general today have to prove to the communities that those years and actions have been in the past and that we all have learned from it.

It will help reduce police brutality if police officers start and remain consistent in treating black people and people of color properly and with compassion. For instance, if a black man is not complying immediately with the police, it will be helpful for the police officer to engage with more words that tell him that his life matters, and maybe it will change his/her heart, and he/she will comply with no incident.

Police can authentically make peace with the people in the communities by doing everything in their power to build future-friendly police and communities by paying more attention to our children, the leaders of tomorrow. Police should make friends with our children by visiting them at school early in life. The police can make it a kind of drill for preschool to kindergarten, maybe once every six months or as they see fit to build a real connection with our children. This will help them to show who they are and that they care about the communities. Police officers should try to leave the children with gifts like books, pencils, and crayons with police drawings, plastic badges, police plastic hats that turn them into mini police officers, police car toys, and police t-shirts or coats. Before you know it, history will be ready for positivity between police officers and the people in the communities. Some of the children may even fall in love with the idea of becoming police officers in the future. This will help in fighting and avoiding police brutality.

Plan for reentry and bail. Some people resist arrest or want to run away when stopped by the police or want to fight their way out because depending on the crime committed, they do not want to go before a judge because they feel they won't get a fair shot at avoiding imprisonment. If a crime is truly committed, the best option is to pay a fine alive, go free, or go to jail alive. Sometimes, crimes are committed by mistake, so instead of running from the police so that you could avoid jail or potentially lose a life, stop, and save your life.

The government should also look into the condition and security in the jail system, making sure that it works, so that people will stop losing their lives unnecessarily in jail or prison. It's supposed to be where people who committed crime could sit down all by themselves, think about what happened, have remorse, and think about what they will do different when they finish their time, not a place to go and die, be taken advantage of, or intimidated by killers, thieves, and sexual predators. The government should also have a kind of compensation for well-behaved prisoners and also have in place a plan for reentry for people who have finished their jail time. For example, a person who committed a crime may be ready to do it again after he comes out from jail because there was no plan in place for reentry. In order for history not to repeat itself, in order to reduce unnecessary assignments for the police, in order to avoid released violent criminals offending and reoffending again, to help reduce police brutality, the government should help by providing them with job opportunities, giving them back their dignity, like permission to have driving licenses commercial licenses, making it easy for them to buy a house, go back to school, learn with private sectors, or give them back their franchise and the right to vote, especially if they behaved well in prison. It will contribute to a calm community and thereby reducing police brutality.

Encouraging people to get out of bail without paying a penny will not reduce police brutality, instead, it will encourage people to continue causing trouble that can lead to police brutality. When you bail people out, they will go ahead and do the worst of their behavior, which leads to people in the community calling the police very often. Sometimes, crime can be mistakenly committed, but when somebody is arrested five times, eight times, seventeen times, or even more just for one person, at times, they end up taking innocent precious lives who want to live their lives to the fullest. At the same time, the police have been called for the same amount of time for the same person, which makes it look like the police have nothing else to do but to answer for one troubled person's call when there are other emergencies where the police are needed. Imagine how many people are living this kind of life. What about the people in those communities? It is disturbing, and this kind of behavior is very abusive to the young minds in the communities. Some children in the neighborhood will think that it is the right way to live life. Therefore, I am calling on our lawmakers to do something about this kind of behavior because it is not helping people in the communities, it jeopardizes them, and it is not helping the police either.

Letting a criminal go free without bail can lead to them returning to the community and committing another crime, possibly even worse than before. The lack of proper sentencing for criminals is not helping the police and the communities. They need to prosecute and put fines or jail time for criminals especially repeat offenders and people with long criminal records should be prosecuted who are killing people and doing other bad things in the communities, such as murderers, rapists, gangs, and abductors.

Children have time-out when they misbehave; therefore, adults should have adult time-out too. People have to make their own choice whether to live peacefully with peacemakers in their own environment long-term or to live with troublemakers in their own environment for a long time.

Legislators should act fast to help with policing in our country. Gangs and domestic terrorism, the unlawful use of force or violence by one person or group of people on humans and their environment within the United States or within a particular country. They perform dangerous acts on human life in violation of the law of the land, bombings, kidnappings, shootouts, killings. This group makes the country feel vulnerable and will face brutality if met with the police officers. To avoid police brutality, one has to avoid these kinds of groups.

DO GOOD IS MY RELIGION

Lastly, as I said earlier, do-good is my religion and solution. I am looking forward to reconciliation and a harmonious world, a world where no one will be treated differently or poorly due to skin color or job title. All I am suggesting is, live and let live with the police and community. No one is supposed to seriously get hurt or die, only because of a stop by the police, including the police officers. Statistics showed that there are more male police officers than female police officers since the beginning of the police force. I believe the hiring more female police officers will help in reducing and avoiding police brutality. In the case of children and women, female police officers will handle it perfectly, as well as when it comes to officers searching female offenders.

A mother can multitask, doing two or three assignments at a time, she can get a no one minute and the next minute she will get a yes by a child. A mother can promise a child heaven and earth in order for the child to make good decisions, but a father will have to repeat it tomorrow for her to believe. A woman can be responsible and emotionally mature. They have the capacity to communicate effectively with people from diverse, social, cultural, and ethnic backgrounds. Women are capable of managing, commanding, inspecting, regulating, and controlling activities. That is why, sometimes, a woman is nicknamed "the boss lady." What a man can do, a woman can do better, all they need is permission, and they will exceed expectations. We need more female police officers, from line operation to supervisory to top command. Women are extremely devoted to their work, whether in uniform or not. They see themselves as mothers first before work. When it comes to handling crying, misery, depression, children, they will jump in as a mother and, at the same time, as a police officer. Increase police professionalism and hire more female police officers today.

Women have played an important role in the world. If a woman can successfully manage a country, a woman can easily handle the police force. These are examples of those type of women; some are with us, and some have passed on: Her Majesty Queen Elizabeth II, London; Angela Merkel, Germany; Margaret Thatcher, United Kingdom; Indira Gandhi, India; Mary Robinson, Ireland; Doris Leuthard, Switzerland; and Mother Theresa.

IN ORDER TO AVOID POLICE BRUTALITY

In order to avoid police brutality, keep police officers for a long time in a community they know and that they are known unless they request a transfer. Avoid too many transfers of police officers in a year. Keep an officer who is doing good in a particular community they serve and start promoting them for doing good community policing in the same community that everybody knows everybody's face. It will help reduce police brutality because it is said, the devil you know is better than the angel you don't know. For example, when I see the police in my city, unless they're new to the area, or if my neighboring police are doing a traffic check at a local checkpoint, I can predict which ones might let you off easily for a small mistake, and which ones I might need to take a different route to avoid.

To avoid police brutality, stay away from anything that will connect you to violence of any kind including gun violence, domestic violence and so on. For any reason if a domestic violence call is made, and the police show up in your house, apartment, workplace or your business place please always keep your two hands up in the air. Please do not reach out for any object for instance a gun or knife. Instead, always, at all times for a peaceful encounter put your hands up for it is dangerous and against the law. Reaching for an object is not an option or solution for the situation. It will be a senseless act of violence holding or waving a weapon, attacking people or police within a domestic call.

To avoid police brutality, do not shoot into people's homes for it may affect innocent creatures or people inside the home.

Also, to avoid brutality, do not forget to abstain yourself from waving a dangerous weapon on the street or anybody can get seriously hurt even police for that kind of behavior can attract police brutality which oftentimes does not end well. When the police are involved like that, always remember to put your hands up in the air as this simple act can save your life.

It's important to remember that only those who are alive can defend themselves and speak for themselves. If someone wants to protect their tree, they should do it while the tree is still standing, not after it has fallen. Similarly, for your own life, if you truly want to protect it, you should take action now while you're still alive, not when it's too late.

STELLA EBURUO

AUTHOR

Stella Eburuo currently lives in Newark, New Jersey with her husband and their three children. She loves family and cherishes people. She obtained a college education Nigeria and worked as a nursing assistant and a cashier.